Family Keepsake Journal

Gigi,
I WANT TO
Hear Your Story

A GRANDMOTHER'S GUIDED JOURNAL
TO SHARE HER LIFE & HER LOVE

"EVERYTHING
I AM
YOU HELPED
ME TO BE."

– RUDYARD KIPLING

THIS BOOK HOLDS THE STORY OF

_____

_____

"GRANDMOTHERS
AND ROSES
ARE MUCH
THE SAME.
EACH IS GOD'S
MASTERPIECE
WITH DIFFERENT
NAMES."

— Author Unknown

TABLE OF CONTENTS

INTRODUCTION

Grandmothers have always been the guardians of our family stories. *Gigi, I Want to Hear Your Story* offers a place for these timeless narrators to share the tales of their journey and reveal the layers of their life.

Imagine journeying with your Gigi, walking alongside her younger self—a dream-filled girl gazing at a sky of possibilities or a spirited teen navigating the bittersweet bridge between innocence and understanding. Each story and tale unveils the many moments and experiences that were knitted together to make her the resilient woman you love and honor.

Gigi, I Want to Hear Your Story isn't just a book or a journal; it's a heartfelt tribute to the age-old tradition of sharing and inheriting the wisdom of those who have lived and experienced life.

And it's a celebration of our amazing grandmothers and all they have done and do to keep our family tied together.

"IT'S SUCH A
GRAND THING TO
BE A MOTHER
OF A MOTHER;
THAT'S WHY
THE WORLD
CALLS HER
'GRANDMOTHER.'"

IT'S YOUR BIRTHDAY

What is your date of your birth?

Month	Day	Year

What time were you born?

____ : ____ AM | PM

What was your full name at birth?

_____

_____

Were you named after a relative or someone else of significance?

_____

_____

If you had been given a vote, what name would you have picked for yourself?

_____

_____

In what city were you born?

_____

Were you born in a hospital? If not, where?

_____

_____

_____

_____

What was your length and weight at birth?

_____

How old were your parents when you were born?

_____

_____

Did your parents have any other children before you? If so, how old were your siblings when you were born?

_____

_____

_____

_____

_____

What were your first words?

_____

_____

How old were you when you started to walk?

_____

What individuals cared for you the majority of the time when you were an infant?

_____

_____

_____

How did your parents describe what you were like when you were a baby?

_____

_____

_____

_____

_____

_____

_____

_____

What stories have you been told about the day you were born?

_____

_____

_____

_____

_____

_____

_____

_____

_____

WHAT HAPPENED THE YEAR YOU WERE BORN

Google the following for the year you were born:

What are a few notable events that occurred that year?

_____

_____

_____

_____

_____

_____

What movie won the Academy Award for Best Picture?

_____

_____

Who won for Best Actor and Best Actress?

_____

_____

What were a few popular movies that came out that year?

_____

_____

_____

_____

_____

What were a few popular songs that came out that year?

_____

_____

_____

_____

_____

_____

What were a few popular television shows?

_____

_____

_____

_____

_____

_____

What were the prices for the following items?

Loaf of bread: _____

Gallon of milk: _____

Cup of coffee: _____

A dozen eggs: _____

First class stamp: _____

Gallon of gas: _____

A movie ticket: _____

The average cost of a new home: _____

"SOME DAYS
I WISH I COULD
GO BACK TO MY
CHILDHOOD.

NOT TO CHANGE
ANYTHING, BUT
TO FEEL A FEW
THINGS TWICE."

- AUTHOR UNKNOWN

CHILDHOOD

What three words or phrases best describe your childhood?

_____

_____

_____

Did you have a nickname when you were growing up? What was it, and how did you get it?

_____

_____

_____

_____

List the activities and sports you participated in.

_____

_____

_____

_____

Did you take music, dance, art, or another type of organized lessons?

_____

_____

_____

_____

What were your regular chores?

_____

_____

_____

Did you receive an allowance? If yes, how much was it?

_____

_____

When you did have money, what did you typically spend it on?

_____

_____

When you were a kid, what did you dream about "becoming" when you grew up?

_____

_____

_____

Who were your best friends during your elementary school days? Are you still in contact with any of them?

_____

_____

_____

_____

_____

If you could be a kid again for one day, what would you spend it doing?

_____

_____

_____

_____

_____

What memories and emotions come forward when you reflect back on your childhood?

_____

_____

_____

_____

_____

_____

_____

_____

_____

_____

WHEN YOU WERE A KID...

What are a few movies you remember loving?

_____

_____

_____

_____

_____

_____

And what songs?

_____

_____

_____

_____

_____

Television shows?

_____

_____

_____

_____

_____

WHEN YOU WERE A KID...

What toys do you remember being especially attached to?

_____

_____

_____

_____

_____

_____

What books were a big part of your childhood?

_____

_____

_____

_____

_____

Any games you remember playing a lot?

_____

_____

_____

_____

_____

"GRANDMOTHER:
A WONDERFUL
MOTHER
WITH LOTS
OF PRACTICE."

– AUTHOR UNKNOWN

THE TEENAGE YEARS

What three words or phrases come to mind when you think back on your teenage years?

_____

_____

_____

How would you describe yourself during this period of your life?

_____

_____

_____

_____

_____

_____

How did you dress and style your hair during your high school years?

_____

_____

_____

_____

_____

Who were your closest friends during these years? When was the last time you spoke with any of them?

_____

_____

_____

_____

_____

What were your parents' opinions on your choice in friends?

_____

_____

_____

Was there a group or activity that your social life and friend group tended to revolve around?

_____

_____

_____

_____

How did you spend a typical weekend night during your high school years?

_____

_____

_____

_____

Is there a specific place where you and your friends would hang out after school or on the weekends?

_____

_____

_____

_____

What was your curfew? How many times did you miss it?

_____

_____

_____

How did your parents respond to your being late?

_____

_____

_____

_____

Did you date during your high school years?

_____

If yes, what was a typical date like for you in those years?

_____

_____

_____

_____

_____

What age were you when you got your driver's license? How many times did you have to take the test to pass?

_____

_____

Who was the primary person who taught you to drive?

_____

_____

What was the make and model of the car you drove in high school?

_____

_____

Did you go to any school dances?

_____

_____

If yes, describe what they were like.

_____

_____

_____

_____

_____

_____

_____

What sports and activities did you participate in during your teens?

_____

_____

_____

_____

What year did you graduate from high school?

_____

How many students were in your graduating class?

_____

Do you remember where in your graduating class you ranked academically?

_____

What were your favorite subjects in school?

_____

_____

_____

_____

And what were your least favorite?

_____

_____

_____

What did you like the most about high school?

_____

_____

_____

_____

_____

_____

Did you ever skip school?

_____

_____

If yes, did you get away with it? What did you do during the time
you should have been in class?

_____

_____

_____

_____

_____

Were there any coming-of-age traditions that you participated
in during your teens or preteens (confirmation, bat mitzvah,
quinceañera, others)?

_____

_____

_____

What jobs did you have during your high school years?

_____

_____

_____

_____

What is something from high school or your teens that you would like a chance to do over?

_____

_____

_____

_____

_____

_____

"TODAY'S TINY LITTLE MOMENTS BECOME TOMORROW'S PRECIOUS MEMORIES."

— Author Unknown

REMEMBERING YOUR TEENAGE BEDROOM:

If you were to give it a name, what would you say was the overall theme of your bedroom?

_____

_____

What were the paint colors of the walls?

_____

_____

What did the bedding look like? What other pieces of furniture did you have besides your bed?

_____

_____

_____

_____

What did you have hanging on the walls?

_____

_____

_____

Describe any additional details about how your teenage bedroom looked and felt.

_____

_____

_____

What advice would you give your teenage self?

_____

_____

_____

_____

_____

What could the teenage version of you teach you today?

_____

_____

_____

_____

Looking back on this time, which moments and experiences stand out as transformative and defining?

_____

_____

_____

_____

_____

_____

_____

WHEN YOU WERE A TEENAGER...

What were a few of your favorite movies?

_____

_____

_____

_____

_____

_____

And television shows?

_____

_____

_____

_____

_____

And books?

_____

_____

_____

_____

_____

_____

WHEN YOU WERE A TEENAGER...

What were your favorite kinds of music?

_____

_____

_____

Your favorite bands or recording artists?

_____

_____

_____

_____

_____

What are a few of your favorite songs from these years?

_____

_____

_____

_____

_____

_____

_____

_____

_____

_____

"ISN'T IT FUNNY HOW DAY BY DAY NOTHING CHANGES, BUT WHEN YOU LOOK BACK EVERYTHING IS DIFFERENT."

– C.S. LEWIS

BECOMING AN ADULT

What did you do after high school? Did you serve in the military, get a job, go to college or a trade school? Something else?

_____

_____

_____

_____

What were your reasons for making these choices?

_____

_____

_____

_____

_____

Looking back, how do you feel now about these decisions?

_____

_____

_____

_____

_____

_____

How did this time period impact who you are today?

_____

_____

_____

_____

_____

_____

_____

If you could go back, what, if anything, would you change about this period of your life?

_____

_____

_____

_____

_____

_____

_____

If you went to college or trade school, what was your major/the focus of your education/training?

_____

_____

_____

Describe what you were like in your 20s.

_____

_____

_____

_____

_____

_____

What were your main goals and priorities during this time?

_____

_____

_____

_____

_____

What advice would you give the 20s version of yourself?

_____

_____

_____

_____

_____

_____

_____

When you reflect on the person you were in your 20s and compare that to who you are today, what core parts of your identity or personality have stayed close to the same?

_____

_____

_____

_____

_____

_____

_____

What has changed?

_____

_____

_____

_____

_____

What was your first major job after high school or college? How old were you? How much were you paid when you started?

_____

_____

_____

_____

Is there a job or profession your parents or family wanted you to pursue? What was it?

_____

_____

When people ask you what profession you are/were in, your response is...

_____

_____

_____

How did you get into this career?

_____

_____

_____

List a few of the work and career-related achievements that you are proudest of.

_____

_____

_____

_____

_____

_____

Where is the first place you lived where you were the one that paid the rent/mortgage? Do you remember the address?

_____

_____

_____

How old were you when you moved here?

_____

Did you live on your own or did you share the place?

_____

_____

What was your share of the rent/mortgage each month?

_____

How long did you live here?

_____

What was your favorite thing about this place?

_____

_____

_____

_____

_____

_____

_____

Describe the place. How many bedrooms and bathrooms did it have? What other things do you remember about it?

_____

_____

_____

_____

_____

_____

_____

What is a favorite memory from your time living there?

_____

_____

_____

_____

_____

_____

_____

_____

_____

_____

_____

"A GRANDMOTHER IS
A LITTLE BIT
PARENT,
A LITTLE BIT
TEACHER,
AND A LITTLE BIT
BEST FRIEND."

– AUTHOR UNKNOWN

YOUR FAMILY

Think back to when you were growing up. What are three words or phrases that best describe your family?

_____

_____

_____

Was your family close-knit with lots of together time, or was it more individualistic with everyone doing their own thing?

_____

_____

How many nights each week on average would your family have dinner together?

_____

_____

When you did eat together, what was the typical routine for how the meal and the time together went?

_____

_____

_____

_____

_____

What did everyone usually talk about?

_____

_____

_____

_____

Who did most of the cooking?

_____

_____

_____

And who did most of the clean up afterwards?

_____

_____

_____

When you were a kid, what were a few of your favorite things that were served for dinner?

_____

_____

_____

_____

_____

_____

And what were the dishes that would make you grimace?

_____

_____

_____

_____

What would happen if you wouldn't eat something?

_____

_____

What holiday was the biggest event for your family when you were growing up?

_____

_____

_____

What are some of the most memorable ways your family would observe this holiday?

_____

_____

_____

_____

_____

_____

_____

How were birthdays, anniversaries, and individual achievements commemorated by your family?

_____

_____

_____

_____

_____

Did your family set aside regular quality time together (things like movie nights or game nights)? If so, write about your memories of these times.

_____

_____

_____

_____

_____

Did you have any relatives who lived nearby that were a big part of your family life?

_____

_____

_____

_____

_____

What role did they have on how you were raised?

_____

_____

_____

_____

_____

What values, beliefs, and rules were strongly emphasized during your upbringing?

_____

_____

_____

_____

_____

What were the expectations and requirements on areas such as grades, chores, and participation in extracurricular activities or sports?

_____

_____

_____

_____

_____

In what ways does the family environment you created for your own kids compare to the one you grew up in?

_____

_____

_____

_____

_____

_____

What were the traditions, rules, and expectations from your childhood that you sought to continue with your kids?

_____

_____

_____

_____

_____

_____

Was there anything you consciously did differently?

_____

_____

_____

_____

_____

"GRANDMOTHERS SPRINKLE STARDUST OVER CHILDREN'S LIVES."

— Alex Haley

In what ways does the family environment you created for your own kids compare to the one you grew up in?

_____

_____

_____

_____

_____

What were the traditions, rules, and expectations from your childhood that you sought to continue with your kids?

_____

_____

_____

_____

_____

Was there anything you consciously did differently?

_____

_____

_____

_____

_____

Time can create changes in perspective. Looking back, how have your views on your upbringing and coming-of-age years changed over time?

_____

_____

_____

_____

_____

_____

_____

What is a favorite memory you have of a time you and your family spent together?

_____

_____

_____

_____

_____

_____

_____

_____

_____

_____

YOUR FAMILY TREE

_____

**MY GREAT-
GRANDMOTHER**

(My Grandmother's Mom)

_____

**MY GREAT-
GRANDMOTHER**

(My Grandfather's Mom)

_____

**MY GREAT-
GRANDFATHER**

(My Grandmother's Dad)

_____

**MY GREAT-
GRANDFATHER**

(My Grandfather's Dad)

_____

MY GRANDMOTHER

(My Dad's Mom)

_____

MY GRANDFATHER

(My Dad's Dad)

_____

MY FATHER

MY GREAT-
GRANDMOTHER
(My Grandmother's Mom)

MY GREAT-
GRANDMOTHER
(My Grandfather's Mom)

MY GREAT-
GRANDFATHER
(My Grandmother's Dad)

MY GREAT-
GRANDFATHER
(My Grandfather's Dad)

MY GRANDMOTHER
(My Mom's Mom)

MY GRANDFATHER
(My Mom's Dad)

MY MOTHER

"FAMILIES ARE LIKE BRANCHES ON A TREE. WE GROW IN DIFFERENT DIRECTIONS YET OUR ROOTS REMAIN AS ONE."

- AUTHOR UNKNOWN

PARENTS & GRANDPARENTS

What was your mother's full name?

_____

Where was she born?

_____

Where did she grow up?

_____

_____

_____

_____

What was your father's full name?

_____

Where was he born?

_____

Where did he grow up?

_____

_____

_____

_____

_____

What three words or phrases best describe your mother?

_____

_____

_____

In what ways are you most like her?

_____

_____

_____

_____

_____

_____

_____

Reflect on and share the qualities and values you most admire in your mother.

_____

_____

_____

_____

_____

_____

_____

What three words or phrases best describe your father?

_____

_____

_____

In what ways are you most like him?

_____

_____

_____

_____

_____

_____

_____

Reflect on and share the qualities and values you most admire in your father.

_____

_____

_____

_____

_____

_____

_____

What was your mother's maiden name?

_____

_____

From what part(s) of the world did your mother's family originate?

_____

_____

_____

What was your father's mother's maiden name?

_____

_____

From what part(s) of the world did your father's family originate?

_____

_____

_____

How did your parents meet?

_____

_____

_____

_____

_____

_____

_____

Do you know their ages when they first met?

_____

_____

When and where were they married? How old was each at the time?

_____

_____

_____

What stories have you been told about their wedding day?

_____

_____

_____

_____

_____

_____

_____

_____

_____

_____

_____

_____

_____

List a few of their hobbies, interests, talents, and skills.

_____

_____

_____

_____

What were their educational backgrounds?

_____

_____

What were your parents' professions?

_____

_____

_____

Did either of them serve in the military?

_____

_____

Parents will often repeat certain "words of wisdom," sayings, and proverbs when giving advice to their kids. What are a few you often heard growing up?

_____

_____

_____

_____

_____

"GRANDMOTHERS ARE JUST ANTIQUE LITTLE GIRLS."

— Author Unknown

Write about a favorite memory of your mother?

Write about a favorite memory of your father?

What were the names of your grandparents on your mother's side of your family?

_____

_____

What was your maternal grandmother's maiden name?

_____

What did you call them?

_____

_____

Where were they born, and where did they grow up?

_____

_____

_____

_____

_____

What was their highest level of education?

_____

_____

What were their professions?

_____

_____

_____

_____

Describe what they were like.

_____

_____

_____

_____

_____

_____

What is a favorite memory of your grandparents on your mom's side?

_____

_____

_____

_____

_____

_____

_____

_____

_____

_____

_____

_____

What were the names of your grandparents on your father's side of your family?

_____

_____

What was your paternal grandmother's maiden name?

_____

What did you call them?

_____

_____

Where were they born and where did they grow up?

_____

_____

_____

_____

What was their highest level of education?

_____

_____

What were their professions?

_____

_____

_____

_____

Describe what they were like.

_____

_____

_____

_____

_____

_____

What is a favorite memory of your grandparents on your father's side?

_____

_____

_____

_____

_____

_____

_____

_____

_____

_____

_____

Did you ever meet your great-grandparents on either side of your family? If yes, what were they like?

What other individuals had a major role in helping you grow up?

What was each one's contribution to who you have become?

_____

_____

_____

_____

_____

_____

_____

_____

_____

_____

_____

_____

_____

_____

_____

_____

_____

_____

_____

"WHAT YOU
ARE IS GOD'S
GIFT TO YOU.

WHAT YOU
BECOME
IS YOUR GIFT
TO GOD."

– HANS URS VON BALTHASAR

YOUR SIBLINGS

Are you an only child, or do you have siblings?

_____

_____

Where are you in the birth order?

_____

_____

List your siblings' names in order of their ages. Be sure to include yourself.

_____

_____

_____

_____

_____

_____

Was life easier or harder for you when you were growing up because of where you fell in the birth order? Why?

_____

_____

_____

_____

What activities or interests did you have in common with each of them?

_____

_____

_____

_____

_____

Which of your siblings were you the closest with when you were young?

_____

_____

Did you look up to any of them?

_____

_____

If yes, write about a time when you did something to impress them or be like them.

_____

_____

_____

_____

_____

_____

What is something you admire about each of your siblings?

Did you share a bedroom with any of them?

_____

_____

_____

If yes, how would you describe the benefits and challenges of the experience?

_____

_____

_____

_____

_____

What is the best part about having a sibling?

_____

_____

_____

_____

_____

_____

_____

_____

_____

_____

What is a memorable story that displays the relationship you and your siblings shared when you were growing up.

"BEING A MOTHER MEANS THAT YOUR HEART IS NO LONGER YOURS; IT WANDERS WHEREVER YOUR CHILDREN DO."

– GEORGE BERNARD SHAW

BECOMING & BEING A MOM

How old were you when you first became a mother?

_____

Think back to the moment when you found out you were pregnant with your first child. Do you remember the first thing you said?

_____

_____

_____

What were your initial thoughts, feelings, and emotions?

_____

_____

_____

Who was the first person you told?

_____

_____

What was their reaction?

_____

_____

_____

_____

Write about the first time you heard your baby's heartbeat or saw them on a sonogram. What was your reaction? Describe your feelings and emotions.

_____

_____

_____

_____

_____

Write about the first time you felt your baby move or kick.

_____

_____

_____

_____

_____

What food cravings did you have?

_____

_____

_____

_____

_____

Write about a particularly memorable, surprising, or humorous moment from each of your pregnancies.

What was your favorite part about being pregnant?

_____

_____

_____

_____

_____

_____

_____

What was the process for selecting your children's names?

_____

_____

_____

_____

Were there any disagreements or negotiations aver any of the names?

_____

_____

_____

_____

_____

What is the inspiration for each of your children's names?

_____

_____

_____

_____

_____

_____

_____

_____

_____

What was the biggest surprise about being a mom that you discovered after your first child arrived?

_____

_____

_____

_____

_____

_____

_____

_____

_____

_____

What were your children's lengths and weights at birth?

_____

_____

_____

_____

How old were they when they took their first steps?

_____

_____

_____

_____

What were their first words?

_____

_____

_____

_____

_____

Is there a special song you would sing or play to your children when they were little?

_____

_____

_____

_____

_____

What tricks would you use to calm them when they were upset?

_____

_____

_____

_____

_____

Are there any specific books you remember reading to your children?

_____

_____

_____

_____

_____

How did having children impact your professional life?

_____

_____

_____

_____

_____

_____

_____

What are the best parts of being a mother?

_____

_____

_____

_____

_____

_____

_____

_____

_____

What advice would you go back and give yourself when you were a new mom?

_____

_____

_____

_____

_____

_____

_____

_____

When you reflect on your life before and after having children, what are the most significant ways becoming and being a mother changed you?

"JUST WHEN YOU THINK YOU KNOW LOVE, SOMETHING LITTLE COMES ALONG AND REMINDS YOU JUST HOW BIG IT IS."

- AUTHOR UNKNOWN

LET'S TALK ABOUT YOUR GRANDKIDS

How old were you when you first became a grandmother?

_____

How many grandkids do you have?

_____

_____

What are your grandkids' names and ages?

_____

_____

_____

_____

_____

How were you told the first time you would be a grandmother?

What was your reaction?

_____

_____

_____

_____

_____

_____

What do you remember about the first time you held your first grandchild?

_____

_____

_____

_____

_____

_____

_____

_____

_____

What is the most surprising thing about being a grandmother?

_____

_____

_____

_____

_____

_____

_____

_____

_____

How is being a grandmother different than being a mother.

_____

_____

_____

_____

_____

_____

_____

_____

_____

_____

_____

_____

_____

_____

_____

_____

_____

_____

_____

_____

"GRANDMA
ALWAYS MADE
YOU FEEL
SHE HAD
BEEN WAITING TO
SEE JUST YOU ALL
DAY AND NOW
THE DAY WAS
COMPLETE."

– MARCY DEMAREE

LOVE & ROMANCE

Do you believe in love at first sight?

_____

Do you believe in soulmates?

_____

What age were you when you went on your first date?

_____

Can you remember who it was with and what you did?

_____

_____

_____

_____

How old were you when you had your first steady relationship?
Who was it with?

_____

_____

Were you ever in a relationship with someone your parents did

not approve of?

_____

_____

Did you have any celebrity crushes when you were young? Who were the most memorable?

_____

_____

_____

When you were younger, did you have "type" you were attracted to? Describe it.

_____

_____

_____

_____

How did you meet our dad?

_____

_____

_____

_____

_____

What was your first impression of him?

_____

_____

_____

_____

_____

How did he ask you out for your first date (or did you ask him)?

_____

_____

_____

What did you do on your first date?

_____

_____

_____

_____

What were your impressions and thoughts about him after that first date?

_____

_____

_____

_____

Do you remember the first time you thought that he might "be the one?" What was it about him or what did he do to help you to feel this way?

_____

_____

_____

_____

_____

How long did you date before you became engaged?

_____

_____

What is your proposal story?

_____

_____

_____

_____

_____

_____

_____

_____

Who as the first person you told that you were engaged?

_____

_____

Describe their reaction.

_____

_____

_____

_____

_____

How much time was there between when you became engaged and the actual wedding date?

_____

_____

What was the process for planning the wedding? Who did most of the work? Were there any challenges?

_____

_____

_____

_____

Did either of you have a bachelor's or bachelorette party? If yes, where was it held?

_____

_____

_____

_____

Where was the wedding held?

_____

_____

_____

How about the reception?

_____

_____

Who were the best man and maid of honor?

_____

_____

Who was in the wedding party?

_____

_____

_____

_____

_____

_____

_____

_____

_____

_____

_____

_____

_____

_____

_____

_____

_____

What was your wedding like? Where was it held and who was there? Any good wedding day stories?

Did you have a honeymoon? If yes, where did you go?

_____

_____

_____

_____

In your opinion, what are the most important qualities of successful and healthy relationship?

_____

_____

_____

_____

_____

_____

_____

How have your relationships helped you be a better person and partner?

_____

_____

_____

_____

_____

_____

_____

This is room to write about any other memories of getting married or additional weddings you may have had.

"LIFE CAN ONLY BE UNDERSTOOD BACKWARDS, BUT IT MUST BE LIVED FORWARDS."

- SOREN KIERKEGAARD

FAVORITES, THOUGHTS, & IDEAS

If you were to write your autobiography, what title would you select to convey and describe your life story?

_____

_____

_____

_____

What is a favorite quote, scripture, or prayer?

_____

_____

_____

_____

_____

What superpower would you choose for yourself?

_____

_____

_____

What is your biggest fear?

_____

_____

_____

If you could live anywhere in the world for a year with all expenses paid, where would you choose?

_____

_____

_____

_____

What is a travel experience that changed your opinions and perspectives about a part of the country or the larger world?

_____

_____

_____

_____

_____

_____

What is a favorite memory of a meal you had while traveling?

_____

_____

_____

_____

_____

_____

What is a favorite travel memory?

Rank in order the top ten places you have you have traveled to:

1. _____

_____

2. _____

_____

3. _____

_____

4. _____

_____

5. _____

_____

6. _____

_____

7. _____

_____

8. _____

_____

9. _____

_____

10. _____

_____

List the top 10 places you would visit if money and time were no concern:

1. _____

_____

2. _____

_____

3. _____

_____

4. _____

_____

5. _____

_____

6. _____

_____

7. _____

_____

8. _____

_____

9. _____

_____

10. _____

_____

What song would you pick as the theme song of your life?

_____

_____

What is a song from your teens that reminds you of a special event or moment from that time? Write about that memory.

_____

_____

_____

_____

_____

In your opinion, which decades had the best music?

_____

_____

How has your taste in music changed over the years?

_____

_____

_____

What was the first concert you attended? Where was it held and when?

_____

_____

_____

What is the first record (or cassette, CD, etc.) you can remember buying or receiving as a gift?

_____

_____

What are a few movies from your childhood and teens that you still enjoy watching?

_____

_____

_____

_____

_____

If you were going to make a movie about your life, what would the title be?

_____

_____

What genre would the movie be?

_____

_____

Who would you cast to play yourself?

_____

How about for the rest of your family?

_____

_____

_____

_____

_____

_____

_____

_____

What are a few television shows and movies that are a must-watch around the holidays?

_____

_____

_____

_____

_____

What television show from the past do you wish was still making new episodes?

_____

_____

How many books would you say you read each year?

_____

_____

How many books would you say you have read in your lifetime?

_____

_____

When you do read, what is your favorite genre?

_____

_____

_____

Do you have a favorite author?

_____

_____

_____

What book or books have majorly impacted the way you think, work, or live your life?

_____

_____

_____

_____

_____

_____

List up to ten of your most favorite books:

1. _____

_____

2. _____

_____

3. _____

_____

4. _____

_____

5. _____

_____

6. _____

_____

7. _____

_____

8. _____

_____

9. _____

_____

10. _____

_____

List up to ten of your most favorite movies:

1. _____

_____

2. _____

_____

3. _____

_____

4. _____

_____

5. _____

_____

6. _____

_____

7. _____

_____

8. _____

_____

9. _____

_____

10. _____

_____

List up to ten of your most favorite songs:

1. _____

_____

2. _____

_____

3. _____

_____

4. _____

_____

5. _____

_____

6. _____

_____

7. _____

_____

8. _____

_____

9. _____

_____

10. _____

_____

List up to ten of your most favorite television shows:

1.

2.

3.

4.

5.

6.

7.

8.

9.

10.

What is a favorite memory from the last twelve months?

_____
_____
_____
_____
_____

What in your life has brought you the greatest joy and contentment?

_____
_____
_____
_____
_____

What are a few personal accomplishments you are especially proud of?

_____
_____
_____
_____
_____
_____
_____

How did you define success for yourself when you were younger?

_____

_____

_____

_____

How do you define success for yourself now?

_____

_____

_____

_____

What do you believe is the purpose of our lives?

_____

_____

_____

_____

Which has the most impact on our lives: fate or free will?

_____

_____

_____

_____

_____

What role did religion have in your family when you were growing up?

_____

_____

_____

_____

_____

_____

_____

Were there any specific religious rituals, celebrations, or traditions that your family observed when you were growing up?

_____

_____

_____

_____

_____

_____

_____

How have your beliefs and practices changed over the course of your life?

_____

_____

_____

_____

_____

_____

_____

_____

_____

What religious or spiritual practices are a part of your life?

_____

_____

_____

_____

_____

_____

_____

_____

_____

Which individuals do you feel especially grateful toward for the role they played in your life story?

_____

_____

_____

_____

_____

_____

What do you do when times are challenging, and you need to find additional inner strength and perseverance?

_____

_____

_____

_____

_____

_____

_____

_____

When you look back over the course of your life, what events and experiences had the biggest impact in shaping the person you are today?

The following pages are for you to expand on some of your answers, to share more memories, and/or to write notes to your loved ones.

_____

_____

_____

_____

_____

_____

_____

_____

_____

_____

_____

_____

_____

_____

_____

_____

_____

_____

At **Hear Your Story**®, we're dedicated to capturing and cherishing life's priceless moments. We passionately believe that within everyone is a treasure of memories and stories that need to be told, cherished, and passed on through generations.

Our journey began from a deeply personal heartache for our founder: watching Alzheimer's steal his father's creativity, curiosity, and memories. From that pain emerged a profound realization - the importance of preserving every precious life story.

Hear Your Story offers more than a beautifully designed journal. We provide a bridge to the past, guiding you or your loved one through cherished memories. It's a gift of reflection, connection, and legacy.

Envision you and your family sitting together as your loved one's journal is shared, smiles everywhere, conversations sparked, and connections deepened. In an age where moments can easily fade, **Hear Your Story** offers something tangible, lasting—a treasured heirloom of life's adventures.

Join us, and let's celebrate every tale. With **Hear Your Story**, no memory goes unheard.

Mom, I Want to Hear Your Story:
A Mother's Guided Journal to Share Her Life and Her Love

Dad, I Want to Hear Your Story:
A Father's Guided Journal to Share His Life and His Love

Grandfather, I Want to Hear Your Story:
A Grandfather's Guided Journal to Share His Life and His Love

Tell Your Life Story:
The Write Your Own Autobiography Guided Journal

To My Wonderful Aunt, I Want to Hear Your Story:
A Guided Journal to Share Her Life and Her Love

To My Uncle, I Want to Hear Your Story:
A Guided Journal to Share His Life and His Love

Mom & Me: Let's Learn Together Journal for Kids

Mother, I Want to Learn Your Recipes
A Keepsake Family Memory Cookbook

Grandmother, I Want to Learn Your Recipes
A Keepsake Family Memory Cookbook

Dad, I Want to Learn Your Recipes
A Keepsake Family Memory Cookbook

Grandfather, I Want to Learn Your Recipes
A Keepsake Family Memory Cookbook

FIND MORE FAMILY CONNECTION AT
hearyourstorybooks   www.hearyourstorybooks.com

Book design by Chelsea Jewell.

ISBN: 978-1-958079-00-3

www.ingramcontent.com/pod-product-compliance
Lightning Source LLC
Chambersburg PA
CBHW070124030426
42335CB00016B/2260